Handy Illinois Genealogy Handbook

Gary L. Morris

©2015 Gary L. Morris

ISBN-13: 978-1508433026

ISBN-10: 150843302X

Table of Contents

Notes

Genealogical Research in Illinois

When Illinois first became a state in 1818, its population was 34,620. It is now the sixth most populous state in America with close to 11.5 million people. You might think it will be hard to find your ancestor among so many people, but don't worry; we'll show you exactly how to track them down. To get you started in tracing your Illinois ancestry, we'll introduce you to the records you'll need, and help you to understand:

1. What they are
2. Where to find them
3. How to use them

These records can be found both online and off, so we'll introduce you to online websites, indexes and databases, as well as brick-and-mortar repositories and other institutions that will help with your research in Illinois. So that you will have a more comprehensive understanding of these records, we have provided a brief history of the "Prairie State" to illustrate what type of records may have been generated during specific time periods. That information will assist you in pinpointing times and locations on which to focus the search for your Illinois ancestors and their records.

A Brief History of Illinois

Illinois was first visited by Europeans in 1673 and the area was claimed by France. The French established a settlement at Cahokia in 1699 and another at Kaskaskia in 1703. French control lasted until 1763 when Illinois was ceded from France to Great Britain. Many settlers from Virginia migrated to the area while it was under British control, which came to an end in 1778 when the militia of George Rogers Clark seized the area. Virginia eventually claimed all land north of the Ohio River, and the first "American" settlement was established at Bellefontaine in 1779.

The introduction of the Northwest Ordinance in 1787 saw French Law repealed and the area organized into counties. Illinois was made part of the Indiana Territory in 1800, and in 1809 it became the Territory of Illinois. Migration to the area continued to increase as fur trappers flocked to the area, and settlements were established in the southern part of the territory, especially around the Wabash and Ohio Rivers and in the Mississippi River Valley. Illinois was finally granted statehood in 1818.

Chicago was founded in 1833 and the final treaty with Native Americans pertaining to Illinois land was signed with the Chippewa, Potawatomi, and Ottawa tribes. The state capital was moved to Springfield in 1839, and the first railroad was opened from the Illinois River to Springfield. In 1844 Joseph Smith, the Mormon prophet, and his brother were killed by a mob at Carthage; prompting a mass exodus of Mormons to an area that we know today as Utah.

The Civil War saw mixed loyalties among the Illinois populace, as many residents had migrated to the area from Virginia, a southern stronghold. The Union though was led by Abraham Lincoln, a native son, and 250,000 troops from Illinois supported the Union cause. In 1865 the Civil War ended, and President Lincoln was assassinated.

Important Dates in Illinois History

1673—Louis Jolliet and Father Marquette arrive in Illinois
1699—Cahokia is founded, the oldest town in Illinois
1717—Illinois becomes part of French Louisiana
1763—England receives Illinois at the end of the French and Indian War
1778—George Rogers Clark captures Kaskaskia from the British
1787—Illinois becomes part of the Northwest Territory
1804—Lewis and Clark expedition starts near Wood River
1809—Illinois Territory is created
1818—Illinois becomes the 21st state
1837—Chicago incorporated as a city
1848—The Illinois & Michigan Canal completed
1871—Fire consumes much of Chicago
1888—Present-day State Capitol built

Famous Battles Fought in Illinois

Illinois has a relatively peaceful history, though there were famous skirmishes between U.S. troops and the Native American tribes in what was known as the **Blackhawk War**. During the Civil war a prisoner of war camp for Confederate soldiers was established at Camp Douglas where many prisoners were starved to death. Death records of the Confederate prisoners who died in Camp Douglas can be viewed online in the **Death Register from Camp Douglas Chicago, Illinois, 1865** held by the National Archives.

The battle accounts can be very effective in uncovering the military records of your ancestor. They can tell you what regiments fought in which battles, and often include the names and ranks of many officers and enlisted men.

Blackhawk War: http://lincoln.lib.niu.edu/blackhawk/

Death Register from Camp Douglas Chicago, Illinois, 1865:
http://research.archives.gov/description/3854696

Common Illinois Genealogical Issues and Resources to Overcome Them

Boundary Changes: Boundary changes are a common obstacle when researching Illinois ancestors. You could be searching for an ancestor's record in one county when in fact it is stored in a different one due to historical county boundary changes. The **Atlas of Historical County Boundaries** can help you to overcome that problem. It provides a chronological listing of every boundary change that has occurred in the history of Illinois.

Atlas of Historical County Boundaries:
http://publications.newberry.org/ahcbp/documents/IL_Consolidated_Chronology.htm#Consolidated_Chronology

Name Changes: Surname changes, variations, and misspellings can complicate genealogical research. It is important to check all spelling variations. Soundex, a program that indexes names by sound, is a useful first step, but you can't rely on it completely as some name variations result in different Soundex codes. The surnames could be different, but the first name may be different too. You can also find records filed under initials, middle names, and nicknames as well, so you will need to **get creative with surname variations** and spellings in order to cover all the possibilities. For help with surname variations read our instructional article on **How to Use Soundex**.

get creative with surname variations:
http://obituarieshelp.org/blog/?p=634

How to Use Soundex: http://obituarieshelp.org/blog/?p=505

Illinois Genealogical Organizations and Archives

Genealogical resources include not only records, but the organizations that house them, or can direct you to them. These institutions include: *Archives, Libraries, Genealogical Societies, Family History Centers, Universities, Churches, and Museums.*

Following are links to their websites, their physical addresses, and a summary of the records you can find there.

Illinois Archives

National Archives and Records Administration – Native American records, naturalizations, court records, service records, immigration records

(NARA)—Great Lakes Region
7358 South Pulaski Road
Chicago, IL 60629-5898
Telephone: 773-948-9019
Fax: 773-948-9050

National Archives and Records Administration:
http://www.archives.gov/chicago/holdings/

Illinois State Archives – military records, Native American records, death indexes, marriage index, court records, servitude and emancipation records, land records

Margret Cross Norton Building
Capital Complex
Springfield, IL 62756
Telephone: 217-782-4682
Fax: 217-524-3930

Illinois State Archives:
http://www.cyberdriveillinois.com/departments/archives/databases/home.html

Illinois State Library - photographs, slides, glass negatives, oral histories, manuscripts and letters, Illinois government documents, Federal government documents, postcards, posters, videos, newspapers, maps

Gwendolyn Brooks Bldg.
300 South Second Street
Springfield, IL 62701-1796
Telephone: 217-785-5600

Illinois State Library:
http://www.cyberdriveillinois.com/departments/library/

Abraham Lincoln Presidential Library – Abraham Lincoln Collection which includes manuscripts, personal papers, letters, and many other documents related to Lincoln and his family, manuscripts, historical newspapers and journals, historical photographs, oral histories, county histories, census records, Native American records, city directories, military records and more

Reference Department
112 No. 6th Street
Springfield, IL 62701-1507
Telephone: 217-524-7216

Abraham Lincoln Presidential Library:
http://www2.illinois.gov/alplm/library/collections/printedmaterials/Pages/default.aspx

Newberry Library - family histories, local histories, probate, deed, court, and tax records, censuses, cemetery records, military rosters, periodicals, genealogical guides, and reference works

The Newberry Library
60 West Walton Street
Chicago, IL 60610
Tel: (312) 943-9090

Newberry Library: http://www.newberry.org/genealogy-and-local-history

Illinois Genealogical and Historical Societies

Genealogical and historical societies have access to extensive catalogues of genealogical data. They are also able to offer expert guidance for genealogical researchers. Many members are professional genealogists who are most willing to share their expertise in finding ancestors.

Illinois State Genealogical Society – death indexes, marriage index, church records, pioneers records, African American resources and more

P.O. Box 10195
Springfield, IL 62791
Telephone: 217-789-1968

Illinois State Genealogical Society: http://www.ilgensoc.org/

Illinois State Historical Society – miscellaneous historical and genealogical resources

210 ½ South Sixth St.
Springfield, IL 62701-2781
Telephone: 217-525-2781
Fax: 217-525-2783

Illinois State Historical Society: www.historyillinois.org/

Decatur Genealogical Society & Library - especially large Genealogical Library containing historical and genealogical information on every county in Illinois

Decatur Genealogical Society
P O BOX 1548
Decatur, IL 62525-1548

Decatur Genealogical Society & Library:
http://www.rootsweb.ancestry.com/~ildecgs/

Illinois Family History Centers

The Family History Centers run by the LDS Church offer free access to billions of genealogical records for free to the general public. They also provide classes on genealogy and one-on-one assistance to inexperienced family historians. Here you will find a **Complete Listing of Illinois Family History Centers**.

Complete Listing of Illinois Family History Centers:
https://familysearch.org/locations/centerlocator

Additional Illinois Genealogical Resources

<u>Illinois Mailing Lists</u>

Mailing lists are internet based facilities that use email to distribute a single message to all who subscribe to it. When information on a particular surname, new records, or any other important genealogy information related to the mailing list topic becomes available, the subscribers are alerted to it. Joining a mailing list is an excellent way to stay up to date on Illinois genealogy research topics. Rootsweb have an extensive listing of **Illinois Mailing Lists** on a variety of topics.

Illinois Mailing Lists:
http://lists.rootsweb.ancestry.com/index/usa/IL/misc.html

<u>Illinois Message Boards</u>

A message board is another internet based facility where people can post questions about a specific genealogy topic and have it answered by other genealogists. If you have questions about a surname, record type, or research topic, you can post your question and other researchers and genealogists will help you with the answer. Be sure to check back regularly, as the answers are not emailed to you. The Illinois message boards at **Rootsweb** are completely free to use.

Rootsweb:
http://boards.rootsweb.com/localities.northam.usa.states/mb.ashx

Illinois Newspapers and Periodicals

Many genealogy periodicals and historical newspapers contain reprinted copies of family genealogies, transcripts of family Bible records, information about local records and archives, census indexes, church records, queries, land records, obituaries, court records, cemetery records, and wills. The following sites have historical Illinois newspapers and periodicals that you can search online or on-site.

Newberry Library - complete runs of many state and county genealogical and historical and publications, as well as important regional and national journals and British journals of local and regional history.

60 West Walton Street
Chicago, IL 60610
Tel: (312) 943-9090

Newberry Library: http://www.newberry.org/genealogy-and-local-history

Illinois Newspaper Project, (University of Illinois at Urbana-Champaign) – microfilmed and digitized newspapers dating from 1865-1922

Illinois Newspaper Project:
http://www.library.illinois.edu/inp/ilhistory.html

GenealogyBank.com – free searchable database of Illinois newspaper archives, 1818-2010

GenealogyBank.com:
http://www.genealogybank.com/gbnk/newspapers/explore/USA/Illinois/

Library of Congress Digital Newspaper Directory – free searchable database of historical U.S. newspapers dating from 1690-present

Library of Congress Digital Newspaper Directory: http://chroniclingamerica.loc.gov/search/titles/

The Online Books Page – links to historical books and periodicals available for viewing online, dating from mid-16th century

The Online Books Page: http://onlinebooks.library.upenn.edu/

NewspaperArchive.com – largest online database of historical newspapers in the world.

NewspaperArchive.com: http://newspaperarchive.com/

Historical Illinois Maps and Gazetteers

Maps are an integral part of genealogical research. They help us to locate landmarks, towns, cities, parishes, states, provinces, waterways and roads and streets. They also help us to determine when and where boundary changes might have taken place, and give us a visualization of the area we're researching in.

For locating place names, a gazetteer is the best possible resource for any genealogist. Gazetteers are also sometimes called "place name dictionaries", and can help you to locate the area in which you need to conduct research. Below are links to the maps and gazetteers for research in Illinois.

Peabody GNIS Service – Illinois:
http://peabody.research.yale.edu/cgi-bin/Query.GNIS?ST=Illinois&SU=1

Color Landform Atlas – Illinois:
http://fermi.jhuapl.edu/states/il_0.html

1985 U.S. Atlas: http://www.livgenmi.com/1895/IL/

Illinois Hometown Locator: http://illinois.hometownlocator.com/

Illinois City Directories

City directories are similar to telephone directories in that they list the residents of a particular area. The difference though is what is important to genealogists, and that is they pre-date telephone directories. You can find an ancestor's information such as their street address, place of employment, occupation, or the name of their spouse. A one-stop-shop for finding city directories in Illinois is the **Illinois Online Historical Directories** which contains a listing of every available city and historical directory related to Illinois.

Illinois Online Historical Directories:
https://sites.google.com/site/onlinedirectorysite/Home/usa/il

Distant Cousin - free searchable online archive of Illinois city directory records and scanned images.

Distant Cousin: http://distantcousin.com/Directories/IL/

Fold3.com - Chicago City Directories 1843-1917, 1923

Fold3.com: http://www.fold3.com/title_22/city_directories_chicago/

Illinois Genealogical Records

<u>Birth, Death, Marriage and Divorce Records</u> – Also known as vital records, birth, death, and marriage certificates are the most basic, yet most important records attached to your ancestor. The reason for their importance is that they not only place your ancestor in a specific place at a definite time, but potentially connect the individual to other relatives. Below is a list of repositories and websites where you can find Illinois vital records

Some county clerks kept vital records as early as 1838. The Family History Library has microfilm copies of these documents for many counties which can be accessed at **Illinois Family History Centers**. Existing originals are found in the county clerk's office or in the **Illinois Regional Archives Depository (IRAD)** for that county.

Illinois Family History Centers:
http://familysearch.org/learn/wiki/en/Category:Illinois_Family_History_Centers

Illinois Regional Archives Depository (IRAD:
http://www.cyberdriveillinois.com/departments/archives/IRAD/

Original copies of Illinois Vital Records for death, birth, marriage, and divorce may be ordered from:

Illinois Department of Public Health
Division of Vital Records
605 West Jefferson Street
Springfield, IL 62702-5097
Telephone: (217) 782-6553
Fax: 217-785-3209

Illinois Department of Public Health:
http://www.idph.state.il.us/vitalrecords/index.htm

The Illinois State Archives has an **Illinois Statewide Marriage Index, 1763–1900** which contains one million marriages, or two million names.

Illinois Statewide Marriage Index, 1763–1900 link to:
http://www.cyberdriveillinois.com/departments/archives/databases/marriage.html

Census Reports

Census records are among the most important genealogical documents for placing your ancestor in a particular place at a specific time. Like BDM records, they can also lead you to other ancestors, particularly those who were living under the authority of the head of household.

Federal census records for Illinois exist from 1800 to 1990. Unfortunately the 1800 census was lost, and the 1810 census contains only a few names from Randolph County. The 1890 census was destroyed, though a few names from Mound Township in McDonough County remain. All other Illinois census records from 1820 to 1930 are available to the public and can be found in the following repositories:

Illinois State Archives – Early census records from 1820-1865

Margret Cross Norton Building
Capital Complex
Springfield, IL 62756
Telephone: 217-782-4682
Fax: 217-524-3930

Illinois State Archives:
http://www.cyberdriveillinois.com/departments/archives/databases/home.html

U.S. National Archives – Federal censuses form 1790-1930

U.S. National Archives: http://www.archives.gov/research/census/

The **Free Census Project** has transcribed many Illinois indexes and new material is added daily

Free Census Project: http://usgwcensus.org/cenfiles/il.htm

Access Genealogy - Illinois census records from 1820-1930

Access Genealogy:
http://www.accessgenealogy.com/census/illinois-census-records.htm

African American Census Schedules Online – slave schedules,
mortality schedules, slave-owners census

African American Census Schedules Online:
http://www.afrigeneas.com/aacensus/

Native Americans in Census Records (US National Archives):
http://www.archives.gov/research/census/native-americans/

Illinois Church Records

Church and synagogue records are a valuable resource, especially for baptisms, marriages, and burials that took place before 1900. You will need to at least have an idea of your ancestor's religious denomination, and in most cases you will have to visit a brick and mortar establishment to view them.

Most church records are kept by the individual church, although in some denominations, records are placed in a regional archive or maintained at the diocesan level. Local Historical Societies are sometimes the repository for the state's older church records. Below are links archives that maintain church records, as well as a few databases that can be viewed online.

The **Family History Library** contains many church records from a variety of denominations on microfilm.

Family History Library:
http://familysearch.org/learn/wiki/en/Family_History_Library

The Illinois State Archives collected some early Illinois church records that are now held by the **Illinois State Library**.

Illinois State Library:
http://www.cyberdriveillinois.com/departments/library/

St. Clair County Genealogical Society (SCCGS) has compiled the **Index to Bethel Baptist Church Minutes and Membership Lists, 1809 - 1909 for St. Clair County, Illinois**

Index to Bethel Baptist Church Minutes and Membership Lists, 1809 - 1909 for St. Clair County, Illinois: http://www.stclair-ilgs.org/bethbpt.htm

Central Repositories for Denominational Records

Most of the records of individual denominations are kept in central repositories. Below is a list of the major congregational archives for Illinois with links to their websites, physical addresses, and contact information.

Baptist

American Baptist Historical Society
1106 South Goodman Street
Rochester, NY 14620
Phone: (716) 473-1740

American Baptist Historical Society: http://abhsarchives.org/

The Church of Jesus Christ of Latter-day Saints (Mormons)

Early, for Mormons in Illinois Wards and Branches can be found on microfilm at the LDS Family History Library in Salt Lake City. The film numbers can be searched online at the **Family History Library Catalog**

Family History Library Catalog:
https://familysearch.org/eng/Library/FHLC/frameset_fhlc.asp

Lutheran

Evangelical Lutheran Church in America (ELCA Archives)
8765 West Higgins Road
Chicago IL 60631-4198
Phone: (800) 638-3522 or (773) 380-2700
Fax: (773) 380-1465

Evangelical Lutheran Church in America (ELCA Archives):
http://www.elca.org/Who-We-Are/History/ELCA-Archives.aspx

Mennonite

Illinois Mennonite Historical and Genealogical Society
675 State Route 116
Metamora, IL 61548-7732
Phone: (309) 367-2551

Illinois Mennonite Historical and Genealogical Society:
http://imhgs.org/.

Methodist

Illinois Great Rivers Annual Conference
United Methodist Church Historical Society
1211 North Park Street
Bloomington, Illinois 61701
Phone: (309) 828-5092, ext. 227

Illinois Great Rivers Annual Conference: http://www.igrc.org/

Garrett Evangelical Theological Seminary
Attn: Archives
2121 Sheridan Road
Evanston, Illinois 60201
Phone: (847) 866-3909

Garrett Evangelical Theological Seminary:
http://www.garrett.edu/

Roman Catholic

Archives of the Archdiocese of Chicago
Joseph Cardinal Bernadine Archive and Record Center
Attn: Assistant Research Archivist
711 West Monroe
Chicago, Illinois 60661
Phone: (312) 831-0711

Archives of the Archdiocese of Chicago:
http://archives.archchicago.org/

Diocese of Belleville
222 South Third Street
Belleville, IL 62220
Phone: (618) 277-8181

Diocese of Belleville:
http://www.diobelle.org/offices/deptinfo.aspx#2

Diocese of Joliet
425 Summit St.
Joliet, IL 60435
Phone: (815) 722-6606

Diocese of Joliet: http://www.dioceseofjoliet.org/

Catholic Diocese of Peoria
419 NE Madison Avenue
Peoria, IL 61603
Phone: (309) 671-1568

Catholic Diocese of Peoria:
http://www.cdop.org/pages/AArchivesOffice.aspx

Diocese of Rockford
555 Colman Center Drive
P.O. Box 7044
Rockford, IL 61108
(815) 399-4300

Diocese of Rockford: http://www.rockforddiocese.org/

Diocese of Springfield
Catholic Pastoral Center
1615 West Washington St.
P.O. Box 3187
Springfield, Illinois 62708-3187
Phone: (217) 698-8500

Diocese of Springfield: http://archives.dio.org/

Illinois Military Records

More than 40 million Americans have participated in some time of war service since America was colonized. The chance of finding your ancestor amongst those records is exceptionally high. Military records can even reveal individuals who never actually served, such as those who registered for the two World Wars but were never called to duty.

Below are a number of links to websites and archives that contain Illinois military records.

Illinois State Archives – Indian War records, Civil War records, Mexican War records, Spanish American War records, War of 1812 Veterans index, muster rolls, and Roll of Honor

Margret Cross Norton Building
Capital Complex
Springfield, IL 62756
Telephone: 217-782-4682
Fax: 217-524-3930

NB: The Illinois State Archives responds only by mail to inquiries, so any telephone, fax, or e-mail inquiries must be accompanied by a mailing address.

Illinois State Archives :
http://www.cyberdriveillinois.com/departments/archives/databases/home.html

U.S. National Archives – WWI Draft registration cards, casualties lists, WWI and WWII service records, Korean War records, Vietnam War records, Civil War and Spanish-American War records, and casualties lists.

U.S. National Archives:
http://www.archives.gov/research/military/veterans/online.html

US Department of Veterans Affairs Nationwide Gravesite Locator – includes information on veterans and their family members buried in veterans and military cemeteries having a government grave marker.

US Department of Veterans Affairs Nationwide Gravesite Locator: http://gravelocator.cem.va.gov/

United States Index to Indian Wars Pension Files, 1892-1926 – military pension records of soldiers who fought in the Indian Wars between 1817 and 1898

United States Index to Indian Wars Pension Files, 1892-1926: https://familysearch.org/search/collection/1979427

United States Registers of Enlistments in the U.S. Army, 1798-1914 - index of men who enlisted in the United States Army, 1798-1914.

United States Registers of Enlistments in the U.S. Army, 1798-1914: https://familysearch.org/search/collection/1880762

United States Mexican War Pension Index, 1887-1926 - index to Mexican War pension files for service between 1846 and 1848

United States Mexican War Pension Index, 1887-1926: https://familysearch.org/search/collection/1979390

Civil War Soldiers Service Records - Service records for both Union and Confederate soldiers indexed by soldier's name, rank, and unit.

Civil War Soldier Service Records: http://go.fold3.com/civilwar_records/

<u>Illinois Cemetery Records</u>

As convenient as it is to search cemetery records online, keep in mind that there are a few disadvantages over visiting a cemetery in person. They are:

- Tombstone information is not always accurately transcribed
- The arrangement of the graves in a cemetery can be crucial as family members are often buried next to each other or in the same grave. This arrangement is not always preserved in the alphabetical indexes that are found online.

With that information in mind, the following websites have databases that can be searched online for Illinois Cemetery records.

Illinois Tombstone Transcription Project - death and burial records

Illinois Tombstone Transcription Project:
http://usgwtombstones.org/illinois/illinois.html

African American Cemeteries Online – African American, slave, and Native American cemetery records

African American Cemeteries Online:
http://africanamericancemeteries.com/

Access Genealogy – huge database of Illinois cemetery record transcriptions

Access Genealogy:
http://www.accessgenealogy.com/cemetery/illinois-cemetery-records.htm

Find a Grave – over 100 million grave records can be searched on this site. Search can be conducted by name, location, or cemetery name.

Find a Grave: http://www.findagrave.com/

Interment.net - A free online database containing approximately 4 million cemetery records from around the world.

Interment.net: http://www.interment.net/

Billion Graves – as the name implies, you can search a billion records including headstone photos, transcriptions, cemetery records, and grave locations.

Billion Graves:
http://billiongraves.com/pages/search/index.php#cemetery

Illinois Obituaries

Obituaries can reveal a wealth about our ancestor and other relatives. You can search our **Illinois Newspaper Obituaries Listings** from hundreds of Illinois newspapers online for free.

Illinois Newspaper Obituaries Listings:
http://obituarieshelp.org/illinois_newspaper_obituaries.html

Illinois Wills and Probate Records

The documents found in a probate packet may include a complete inventory of a person's estate, newspaper entries, witness testimony, a copy of a will, list of debtors and creditors, names of executors or trustees, names of heirs. They can not only tell you about the ancestor you're currently researching, but lead to other ancestors. Most of these records must be accessed at a county court or clerk's office, but some can be found online as well. You can obtain copies of the original probate records by writing to the county clerk.

Since 1964, the circuit court in each county has custody of the earlier court records including those of the former Cook County Superior Court and a few other Chicago area courts. They can be found at:

Clerk of Circuit Court
Archives Room 1113
Richard J. Daley Center
50 W. Washington St.
Chicago, IL 60602
Telephone: 312- 603-6601
Fax: 312-603-4974

Clerk of Circuit Court:
http://www.cookcountyclerkofcourt.org/?RecArchivePage=6000&section=RecArchivePage

The **Illinois Regional Archives** has a huge database of court and county records for the entire state of Illinois

Illinois Regional Archives:
http://www.cyberdriveillinois.com/departments/archives/databases/home.html

Family Search – has an online collection of probate records, which includes will, indexes, dating from 1819-1970

Family Search: https://familysearch.org/search/collection/1834344

Illinois Immigration and Naturalization Records

The naturalization process generated many types of records, including petitions, declarations of intention, and oaths of allegiance. These records can provide family historians with information such as a person's birth date and place of birth, immigration year, marital status, spouse information, occupation, witnesses' names and addresses, and more.

US National Archives – Immigration and Naturalization records for the entire United States

US National Archives:
http://www.archives.gov/research/immigration/passenger-arrival.html

Family Search has two searchable online indexes, the **Illinois, Northern District (Eastern Division), Naturalization Index, 1926-1979**, and the **Illinois, Northern District Naturalization Index, 1840-1950**

Illinois, Northern District (Eastern Division), Naturalization Index, 1926-1979:
https://familysearch.org/search/collection/2040533

Illinois, Northern District Naturalization Index, 1840-1950 link to: https://familysearch.org/search/collection/1838804

Illinois Native American Records

Access Genealogy – Illinois Native American census records, tribal histories, and much more

Access Genealogy: http://www.accessgenealogy.com/native/illinois-indian-tribes.htm

U.S. National Archives - information on American Indians who maintained their ties to Federally-recognized Tribes (1830-1970).

U.S. National Archives: http://www.archives.gov/research/native-americans/

Records of the Bureau of Indian Affairs (BIA) link to: **http://www.archives.gov/research/guide-fed-records/groups/075.html**

American Indians Records Repository - records dating from the 1700s including trust, education and other historic Indian Affairs records

American Indian Records Repository
Meritex Enterprises
17501 West 98th Street
Lenexa, KS 66219
Phone: 913-888-0601

American Indians Records Repository: http://www.doi.gov/ost/records_mgmt/american-indian-records-repository.cfm

Missing Matriarchs – Resources for Researching Female Illinois Ancestors

Looking for female ancestors requires an adjustment of how we view traditional records sources. A woman's identity was often under that of her husband, and often individual records for them can be difficult to locate. The following resources are effective in locating female ancestors in Illinois where traditional records may not reveal them.

Marriage and Divorce Records

Marriages have been recorded in county records since 1791. The Illinois State Archives has copies of county marriage records from 1791-1920. The first divorces were granted in 1809 and those records have been kept by the county clerks and the clerk of the Superior Court in Cook County. Many county records have been filmed such as:

1. Gallatin County Clerk marriage certificates, 1813-1896 (film 0969484 ff.) at the Gallatin County Courthouse in Carbondale
2. Randolph County clerk marriage records, 1807-1927 (film 0975007 ff.) at the Randolph County Courthouse in Chester
3. Cook County Clerks marriage licenses, 1871-1920, and marriage index, 1871-1916 (film 1288817 ff.) at the Cook County Courthouse in Chicago
4.

Bibliographies

- *Resources for the Study of Women's History Located in the Illinois Historical Survey Library,* Nelson Beck (Illinois Historical Survey Library, 1979)
- *The Women of Illinois,* Henry McCormick (Library of Congress film 1674246)
- *Somewhere in Between: Quilts and Quilters of Illinois*, Rita Barrow Barber (American Quilters Society, 1986)
- *The Roads They Made: Women in Illinois History,* Adele Mitchell and Marlene Steen Wortman (Charles H. Kerr, 1972)

Selected Resources for Illinois Women's History

Chicago Area Women's History Conference
400 E. Randolph, #3910
Chicago, IL 60601

Daughters of Union Veterans of the Civil War
503 S. Walnut St.
Springfield, Il 62704

Helen Matthes Library
100 Market St.
Effingham, IL 62401

Common Illinois Surnames

The following surnames are among the most common in Illinois and are also being currently researched by other genealogists. If you find your surname here, there is a chance that some research has already been performed on your ancestor.

Abernathy, Albertson, Andersen, Archer, Austin, Baer, Bearsley, Boyd, Brown, Bryson, Buchholz, Burger,Christensen, Clements, Cordani, Coyle, Davidson, Diestelmeier, Eckert, Edwards, Everly, Farthing, Fields, Forth, Frigo, Gammon, Garrison, Gibson, Good, Hamill, Harris, Hartstone, Hatahet, Hess, Hill, Hoover, Hughes, Jackson, Jones, Joynt, Judge, Kelsey, Klitz, Knight, Kruegel, Krug, Lablaiks, Lane, Locke, Lockwood, Lundblade, Marshel, Masterman, Mayberry, McCormick, Millenbine, Miller, Montgomery, Neel, Newman, Nilles, Norris, Olerud, Ore, Palmer, Penhollow, Puetz, Rainey, Reuter, Reynolds, Rodhisel, Rosbrook, Shaub, Sikkema, Stannard, Strange, Swarthy, Tennison, Thompson, Tompkins, Trammel, Trotter, Watson, Weier, Westfall, Wheeler, Whipple, Wilson, Woodyatt, Wright, Wyatt, Yarbor, Young, Youngblood

About the Author

Gary L. Morris worked from 2009 to 2014 as a professional researcher for a major player in the genealogy field. After tracing his family lineage back to 1683, he found that genealogy could be an expensive undertaking. As such, has decided to publish these helpful guides to share the valuable free information he has discovered during his career to help others trace their family lineages as inexpensively as possible. An avid genealogist himself, he hopes you will find this guide factual, thorough, helpful, and most of all, effective in helping you to find your family members.

Notes

Notes

www.ingramcontent.com/pod-product-compliance
Lightning Source LLC
Chambersburg PA
CBHW070517290526
45790CB00003B/1243